SRA Reading Mastery®
Transformations

Reading
Textbook C

Siegfried Engelmann

Owen Engelmann

Karen Davis

Mc
Graw
Hill

Acknowledgments

The authors are grateful to the following people for their assistance in the preparations of Reading Mastery Transformations Grade K Reading.

Joanna Jachowicz   Cally Dwyer
Blake Engelmann   Melissa Morrow
Charlene Tolles-Engelmann Toni Reeves

Emily Jachowicz for her valuable student input.

We'd also like to acknowledge, from McGraw Hill, the valuable contributions by:

Mary Eisele
Nancy Stigers
Jason Yanok

PHOTO CREDITS

L144 Page 129 (sea lion)AlexGoldblum/Getty Images (sea turtle)Kjeld Friis.dk/Getty Images **L144 Page 130** (shark)NOAA (whale)James R.D. Scott/Getty Images (goldfish)Anthony Bradshaw/Getty Images **L144 Page 131** (whale shark)Krzysztof Odziomek/Shutterstock **L156 Page 174** (hummingbird)Larry Selman/MostlyBirds.com/Getty Images (eagle)Ken Canning/Getty Images (crow)Eric Isselee/123RF (ducks)Peter Radosa/123RF **L156 Page 175** (gull)gekaskr ©123RF.com (ostrich)Paul Lovichi Photography/Alamy Stock Photo **L156 Page 176** (peacock)ksushsh/iStock/Getty Images **L156 Page 176** (birds)Jyotirmoy Golder/Shutterstock (eggs)Image Source **L157 Page 179** (osprey)Craig Hanson/Shutterstock (gull)Pixtal/age fotostock **L157 Page 180** (swallows)Photo by Michael Russell/Moment Open/Getty Images (storks)okcid/123RF (eggs)Viktor Sergeevich/Shutterstock **L158 Page 183** (pea pod) Shutterstock/Danny Smythe (corn kernels)Siede Preis/Getty Images (beans)Shutterstock/MRS. Siwaporn (corn)Renee Comet/National Cancer Institute (NCI) (bean pod)Maxim Tatarinov/123RF

(green beans)smereka/Shutterstock **L158 Page 184** (corn)YinYang/Getty Images (corn ear) Bryan Mullennix/Pixtal/age footstock (popcorn) McGraw Hill **L158 Page 185** (seed) serezniy/123RF (sprout)Peter Lewis/123RF (seedling) Denis and Yulia Pogostins/123RF (bean plant) phana sitti/123RF **L159 Page 187** (corn) Bryan Mullennix/Pixtal/age footstock (bean) lynx/iconotec.com/Glow Images **L159 Page 188** (wheat)Bear Dancer Studios/Mark Dierker (rice)Korradol Yamsattham/123RF **L159 Page 189** (field)Michal Rosenstein/123RF (wheat ears) Oksana Tkachuk/123RF (wheat seeds)McGraw Hill/Jacques Cornell (bread)Everyday Images/ Alamy (baking ingredients)McGraw Hill (pancakes)bellanatella/123RF **L159 Page 190** (soil/ seeds)ligora/iStock/Getty Images (field)Leonid Eremeychuk/123RF (wheat ears)lynx/iconotec. com/Glowimages **L159 Page 191** (rice paddy)Wasana Thongton/EyeEm/Getty Images (rice seedling)Nuttapong Wongcheronkit/Alamy Stock Photo (rice stalk)frameangel/123RF (rice cooker)McGraw Hill

mheducation.com/prek-12

1. <u>wh</u>y
2. <u>whil</u>e

1. div e
2. hiv e
3. mor e
4. sor e

1. tal e
2. bik e
3. back
4. s<u>ea</u>
5. thing

1. <u>other</u>
2. be
3. by
4. <u>t</u>ears

1. it's
2. can't

The Hill of Mud
Part 3

Bob played and played in the mud. At last some of his pals told him, "It's late. You must run to be home by five."

As Bob ran home, a man said, "I see a hill of mud that can run."

Bob made it home by five. His dad said, "But you didn't stay near the path." So Bob can't hike with his pals for some time.

The end.

3

1. <u>wh</u>eel
2. <u>wh</u>ile
3. <u>wh</u>y

1. <u>g</u><u>ear</u>
2. r<u>ear</u>
3. h<u>ear</u>
4. dry
5. cry

1. things
2. bug
3. back
4. fill<u>ed</u>

1. tales
2. rode
3. s<u>ea</u>
4. waves
5. sore
6. bikes

We Like That

We can hike and we can bike.
And we can do things that we like.
We may play and we may run.
Or we may read to have some fun.
If it is dry, we can bike to the sea.
We see big waves as we sit near a tree.
We come back home filled with tales
Of stones and waves and sea and sails.

We Like That

We can hike and we can bike.
And we can do things that we like.

We may play and we may run.
Or we may read to have some fun.
If it is dry, we can bike to the sea.
We see big waves as we sit near a tree.

We come back home fill<u>ed</u> with tales
Of stones and waves and <u>sea</u> and s<u>ai</u>ls.

113

1. **wh**eel
2. **wh**y
3. **wh**ile

1. **t**ear
2. **g**ear
3. **r**ear
4. **d**ear
5. **h**ear

1. hive
2. games
3. bikes
4. bug

1. rode
2. bee
3. Ann
4. some
5. sore

Ann and Bob discussed trees.

Note to Dad

Dear Dad,

    The other day we rode bikes to a lake. We ate and played games. I had my gear near a bee hive. Bees gave me some tears. I have a sore ear, but I can hear. And I have a sore rear. So I can't sit. And I can't ride my bike for a while.

               From Ann

Note to Dad

Dear Dad,
   The other day we rode bikes to a lake. We ate and played games.

I had my gear near a bee hive. Bees gave me some tears.

I have a sore ear, but I can hear. And I have a sore rear. So I can't sit. And I can't ride my bike for a while.

From Ann

114

1. home
2. this
3. while
4. holes
5. hat

1. at<u>e</u>
2. w<u>ai</u>t
3. rode
4. t<u>oa</u>d
5. jok<u>e</u>
6. s<u>oa</u>k

1. <u>ea</u>t
2. at
3. bugs
4. jump

The Bug and the Toad

A toad had a fine home. A mean bug dug a big hole into the home.

The toad said, "This is my home. Don't make holes in it."

The bug said, "I can make holes if I feel like it."

The toad said, "And I can eat bugs if I feel like it."

And the toad did that.

The end.

20

115

1. <u>a</u>rm
2. f<u>a</u>rm
3. b<u>ar</u>n

1. to
2. do
3. who

1. w<u>ai</u>t
2. c<u>oa</u>t
3. l<u>ea</u>p
4. s<u>oa</u>k
5. h<u>ea</u>r
6. r<u>ai</u>ns

1. blow
2. jump
3. wind
4. lick
5. it's

The old man was greedy.

21

I Wait for My Pal

I hate to wait. But I have to sit and wait while it rains.

I wait for my pal, the mail man.

The rain has made him late. That rain will soak my coat and my tail, but I will sit in the rain.

At last I hear him and see him. I will jump up. It's time for us to have some fun.

116

1. b<u>ar</u>n
2. <u>ar</u>t
3. st<u>ar</u>t

1. wh<u>o</u>
2. d<u>o</u>

1. three
2. rug
3. stick
4. stove
5. but

1. aw<u>ay</u>
2. fire
3. last
4. flame

1. c<u>ar</u>
2. f<u>ar</u>
3. dry
4. sky

25

Fun with My Pal

I sat in the r<u>ai</u>n, but at last my pal came home. We had fun as we pl<u>ayed</u> with a stick. We pl<u>ayed</u> in the r<u>ai</u>n.

He told me it was time to eat. We ate near the stove in his home.

At last I am dry. So I go to the rug. I can h<u>ea</u>r the r<u>ai</u>n, but I am dry. And it is time for me to sleep.

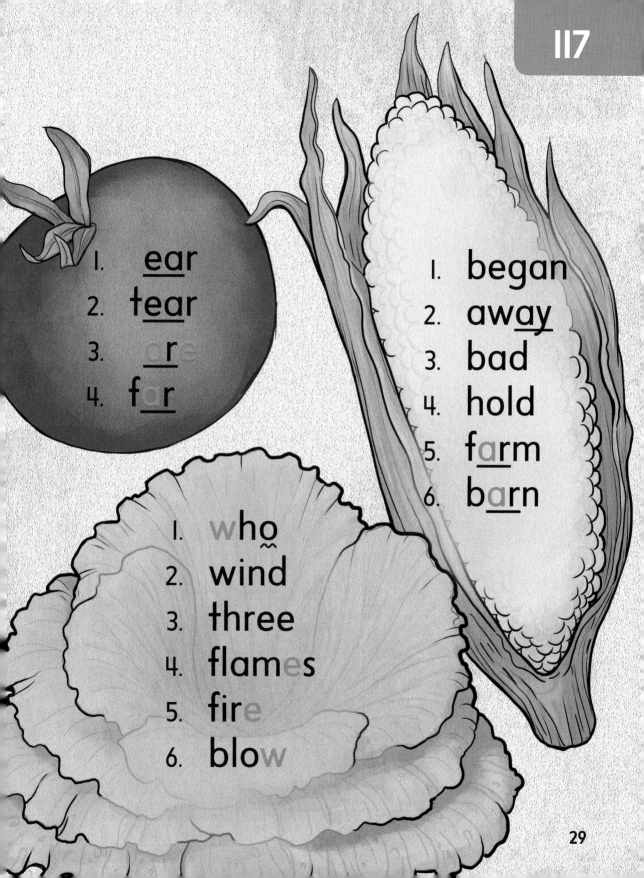

117

1. <u>ea</u>r
2. t<u>ea</u>r
3. <u>a</u>re
4. f<u>ar</u>

1. began
2. aw<u>ay</u>
3. bad
4. hold
5. f<u>ar</u>m
6. b<u>ar</u>n

1. who
2. wind
3. three
4. flames
5. fire
6. blow

29

A Mean Wind
Part 1

A mean wind made three pals cold. So the pals made a fire near a farm. The mean wind said, "I will blow and make that fire big." The wind made flames leap way up.

The pals said, "We have to keep this fire from the barn." But the pals didn't hold the fire. And in no time, that fire was near the barn.

More to come.

A Mean Wind
Part 1

A mean wind made three pals cold. So the pals made a fire near a farm.

The mean wind said, "I will blow and make that fire big." The wind made flames leap way up.

The pals said, "We have to keep this fire from the barn." But the pals didn't hold the fire. And in no time, that fire was near the barn.

118

1. <u>a</u>re
2. r<u>ea</u>r
3. r<u>oa</u>r
4. <u>a</u>rm
5. f<u>ea</u>r

1. <u>wha</u>t
2. aw<u>ay</u>
3. side
4. lick

1. sky
2. ho ho
3. bad
4. slide

1. said
2. you
3. was
4. to
5. who

34

A Mean Wind
Part 2

A mean wind made a fire leap over to a barn. The wind made a bad joke. The wind said, "Ho ho. It's time for a barn fire."

The pals said, "If we don't hold this fire, the barn will go up in flames."

The mean wind said, "You can't keep these flames away from the barn." And the wind made the fire jump up and lick at the barn.

More to come.

If we don't hold this fire, the barn will go up in flames.

1. f**ear**
2. f**ar**
3. t**ear**
4. t**ar**

1. wi**sh**
2. fi**sh**
3. **sh**e

1. won't
2. sid**e**
3. slid**e**
4. sky
5. s**oa**k
6. miss

1. **what**
2. on
3. began
4. aw**ay**
5. just

A Mean Wind
Part 3

The mean wind said, "I will blow big flames up the side of that barn."

But as the flames began to leap up the side of the barn, rain came from the sky.

The r<u>ai</u>n said to the m<u>ea</u>n wind, "I will keep those flames aw<u>ay</u> fr͜om the b<u>ar</u>n."

In no time, the fire was no more.

The rain told the wind, "Leave this farm or I will soak you some more."

The pals said, "We like rain."

But the mean wind said, "I hate rain."

The end.

1. <u>sh</u>ip
2. <u>sho</u>w
3. wi<u>sh</u>
4. <u>sh</u>e

1. <u>wh</u>at
2. who
3. on
4. no
5. rug
6. h<u>ar</u>d

1. slide
2. slid
3. hate
4. hat
5. fast
6. won't

The Fast Rug
Part 1

A hard rain made mud on a hill. A pig told a goat, "We can have some fun on that hill. We can sit in the mud and slide."

44

The g<u>oa</u>t said, "But we will
hav<u>e</u> mud on us. I don't like
mud."

The pig said, "I hav<u>e</u> a rug.
We can sit on the rug. That rug
will slide on the mud. And we
won't hav<u>e</u> mud on us."

So the g<u>oa</u>t and the pig sat on that rug. The pig said, "Hold on." And the rug slid on the mud. The g<u>oa</u>t said, "This rug is fast."

More to come.

122

1. she
2. ship
3. cash

1. ring
2. sing

1. to
2. too
3. do
4. under
5. oh

1. snake
2. land
3. slid
4. stuck
5. free
6. still

1. miss
2. on
3. sailed

47

The Fast Rug
Part 2

A goat and a pig sat on a rug. That rug slid on the side of a hill. It slid fast. The goat said, "A tree is in the way."

A tree is in the way.

The pig said, "We will miss that tree." But the rug ran into that tree. The g<u>oa</u>t and the pig s<u>ai</u>l<u>ed</u> into the sky. <u>Wha</u>t did the pals land in? Mud, mud, mud.

Oh d<u>ea</u>r.

The goat said, "I hate mud, but we have mud on us. So we can slide on the mud some more." Did the pals do that? Yes.

The end.

Weeeee.

1. **sh**am**e**
2. ca**sh**
3. wi**sh**

1. to
2. too
3. two
4. won't
5. the big one
6. wise

1. have
2. stuck
3. free
4. still
5. spoke
6. oh

1. sing
2. ring
3. bring
4. thing

The Mole and the Crow
Part One

Moles can't see. A mole dug a hole and ran into a tree. The mole asked the tree, "Who are you?" The tree was still.

A crow was in the tree. That crow said, "I will have some fun with that mole."

The crow said, "Oh, mole. You have run into me. I am the big one. And I am stuck in the mud. Can you dig and free my feet?"

"I don't know," the mole said. "But I will try."

More to come.

124

1. <u>shin</u>e
2. <u>fish</u>
3. <u>sh</u>e

1. pl<u>ay</u>ing
2. trying
3. digging

1. thes e
2. while
3. will
4. snak e
5. think

1. her
2. w<u>er</u>e
3. <u>o</u>th<u>er</u>
4. m<u>o</u>th<u>er</u>

1. tw<u>o</u>
2. wis e
3. fr<u>o</u>m

The Mole and the Crow
Part Two

A crow made a mole think that a tree was the big one. The crow asked the mole to dig and free his feet. So the mole began to dig. The mole dug and dug. At last, the mole said, "I dig, dig, dig, but these feet are big, big, big."

As the mole dug, she came to the home of a wise old snake. The snake said, "Why do you dig into the side of my home?"

The mole said, "I need to free these big feet from the mud."

"What big feet?" the snake asked. The mole told the snake.

> More to come.

58

125

1. from
2. of
3. one
4. know
5. for
6. free

1. wer<u>e</u>
2. h<u>er</u>
3. und<u>er</u>

1. trying
2. pl<u>ay</u>ing
3. digging

1. <u>sh</u>ow
2. <u>sh</u>ame
3. ca<u>sh</u>

1. think
2. thing
3. lump
4. gold

The Mole and the Crow
Part Three

The mole was trying to free feet. The mole dug into the home of a wise old snake. The snake told the mole, "You think you are digging under the big one. But you are digging under a tree."

The mole said, "But the big one told me what to do."

"No," the snake said. "Some one is playing a joke."

"What can I do?" the mole asked.

The snake smiled and said, "I think I know what to do. We can play jokes, too. And I think I know a fine joke."

More to come.

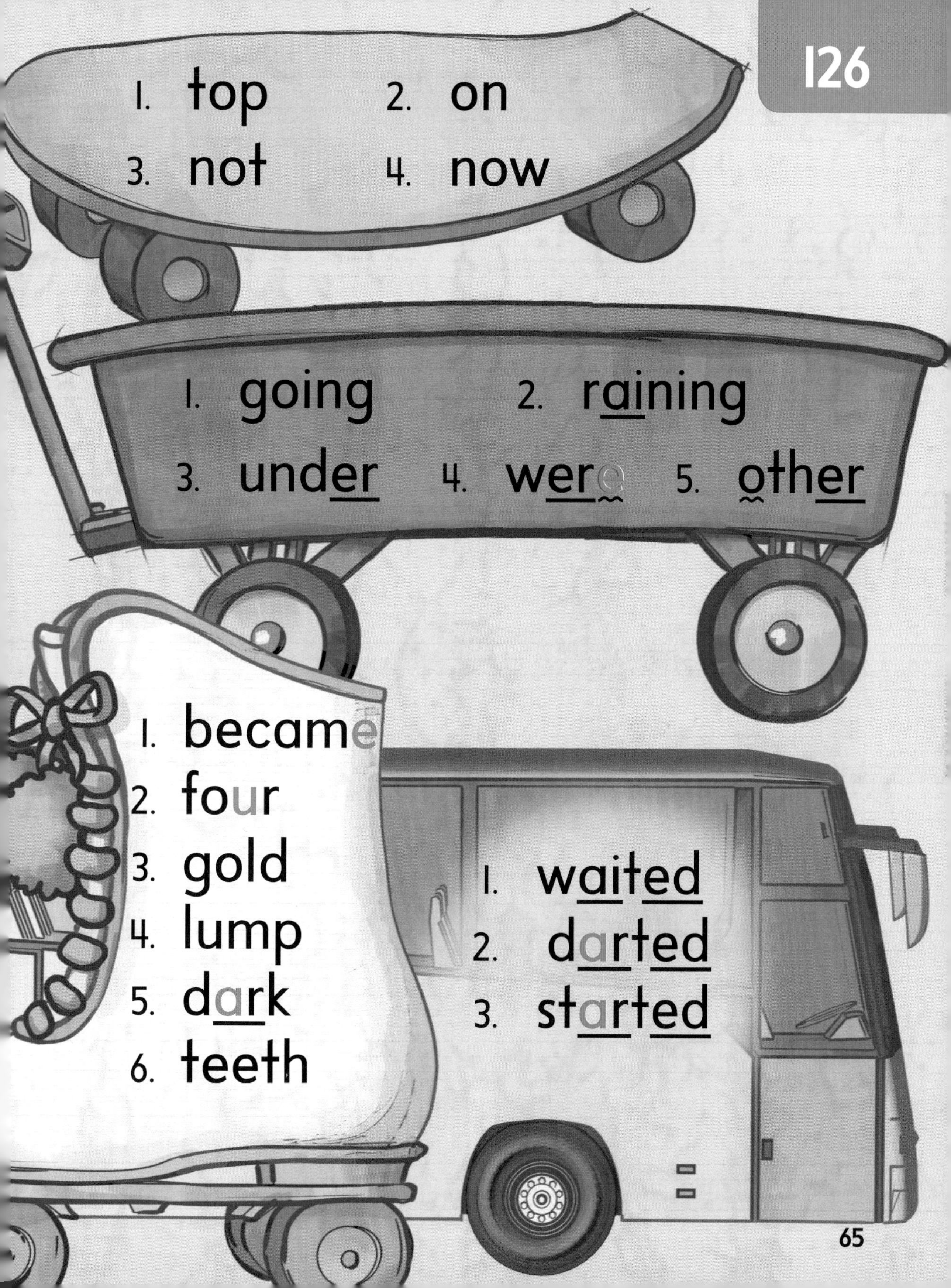

126

1. top
2. on
3. not
4. now

1. going
2. raining
3. under
4. were
5. other

1. became
2. four
3. gold
4. lump
5. dark
6. teeth

1. waited
2. darted
3. started

The Mole and the Crow
Part Four

The wise old snake told the mole what to do. The mole came from the hole. She said to the crow, "Oh, big one, I can't free feet that are stuck in gold."

"What did you say?" the crow asked.

The mole told the crow, "Just go into the hole I was digging. You will see gold at the back of the hole."

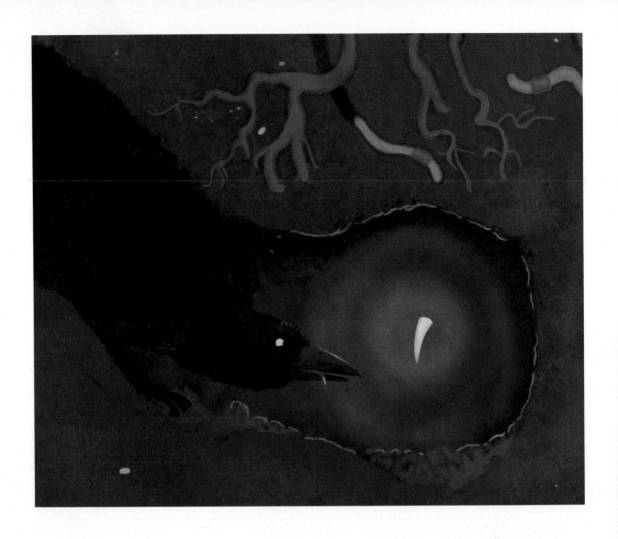

So the crow slid into the hole the mole had dug. At last the crow came to a lump of gold.

One part to go.

127

1. lot
2. how
3. not
4. stop

1. st<u>ar</u>ted
2. d<u>ar</u>ted
3. hat<u>e</u>d

1. spok<u>e</u>
2. <u>sh</u>am<u>e</u>
3. d<u>ar</u>k
4. becam<u>e</u>
5. pl<u>ay</u>ing
6. grab

1. teeth
2. sing
3. think
4. must

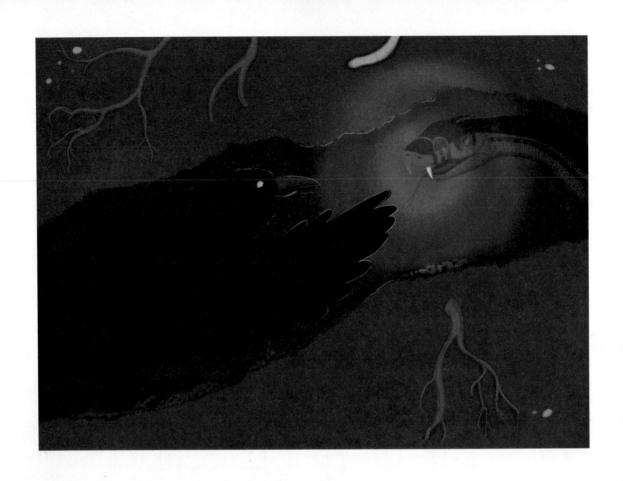

The Mole and the Crow
Part Five

"I see gold," the crow said. She was in the hole. As she started to grab for the gold, it became dark. The crow didn't know it, but the gold was one of the snake's gold teeth.

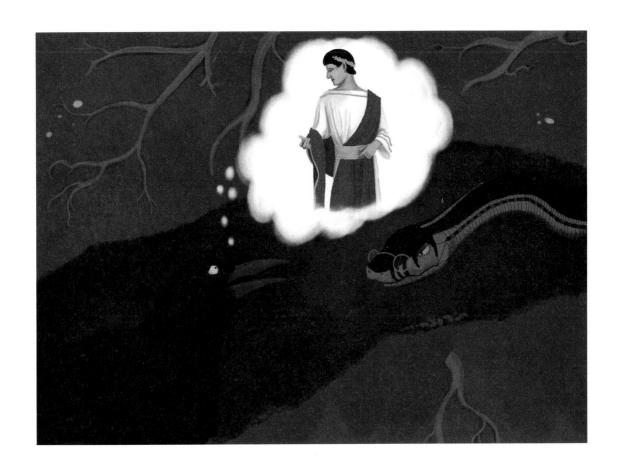

The snake spoke like the big one.
"Oh, bad crow," he said. "Shame on
you for playing mean jokes. It was
bad to make the mole think my feet
are stuck in mud."

You can have the gold.

The crow darted from the hole. As she started to fly away, she said to the mole, "The big one is mad at me. I must leave here. You can have the gold."

That was the last joke the crow played on moles.

The end.

o   th   er   sh   ar

1. got
2. lot
3. cow
4. now
5. stop

1. end<u>ed</u>
2. land<u>ed</u>
3. need<u>ed</u>

1. wins
2. w<u>a</u>iting
3. eating
4. singing
5. fast<u>er</u>

1. corn
2. Jan
3. greet
4. ov<u>er</u>
5. m<u>o</u>th<u>er</u>
6. aw<u>ay</u>

What Jan Sings

Jan liked to sing, but she made her mother sick of her singing.

One day her mother spoke to Jan. Her mother said, "I like the way you sing, but you sing the same thing over and over. Can you sing other things?"

Jan said, "I like to sing the same thing."

Her mother said, "I will do some thing for you if you sing more than one thing. What can I do for you?"

Jan said, "Will you sing with me?"

Jan's mother said, "Yes."

Now Jan and her mother sing lots of fine things. If you are near Jan's home, you can hear that singing.

The end.

<u>Wh</u>at Jan Sings

Jan lik<u>ed</u> to sing, but <u>she</u> made h<u>er</u> m<u>o</u>th<u>er</u> sick of h<u>er</u> singing.

<u>O</u>ne d<u>ay</u> h<u>er</u> m<u>o</u>th<u>er</u> spoke to Jan. H<u>er</u> m<u>o</u>th<u>er</u> said, "I like the w<u>ay</u> you sing, but you sing the same thing ov<u>er</u> and ov<u>er</u>. Can you sing <u>o</u>th<u>er</u> things?"

Jan said, "I like to sing the same thing."

Her m̯othe̯r said, "I will do̯ so̯me
thing for you if you sing more than
o̯ne thing. W̲h̯a̯t can I do̯ for you?"
    Jan said, "Will you sing with me?"
    Jan's m̯othe̯r said, "Yes."

Now Jan and h<u>er</u> m<u>other</u> sing lots of fine things. If you <u>are</u> n<u>ear</u> Jan's home, you can h<u>ear</u> that singing.

The end.

1. got
2. cow
3. <u>sh</u>op
4. not

1. end<u>ed</u>
2. hat<u>ed</u>
3. hand<u>ed</u>

1. corn
2. leap
3. over
4. away
5. thes<u>e</u>

1. wins
2. eating
3. fast<u>er</u>
4. thinks
5. lat<u>er</u>

1. too   2. two   3. who

Eating Corn

A pig and a goat liked to eat. One day, the goat and the pig were near a pile of corn.

The goat said, "I can eat that pile of corn."

The pig said, "Me too."

The goat got mad and said, "I can eat faster than you."

Now the pig said, "You can not."

A cow said, "Why don't the two of you start eating and see who wins?"

So the goat and the pig started to eat the corn.

The cow said, "I think I will eat, too." And she did.

Who ate more corn? The cow.
Who ate faster? The cow.
Who got mad? The pig and the goat.

The end.

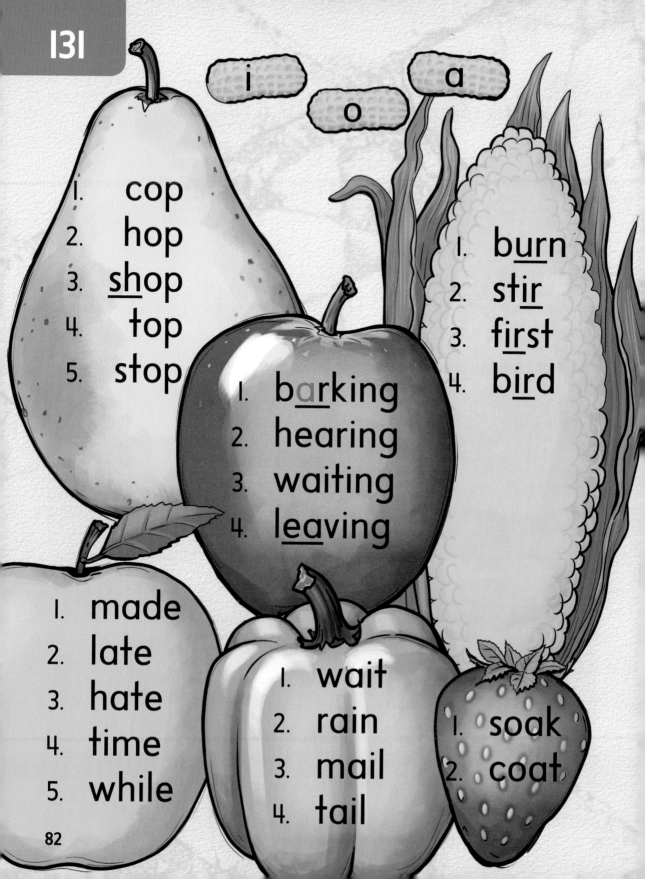

131

i

o

a

1. cop
2. hop
3. <u>sh</u>op
4. top
5. stop

1. b<u>ur</u>n
2. st<u>ir</u>
3. f<u>ir</u>st
4. b<u>ir</u>d

1. b<u>a</u>rking
2. hearing
3. waiting
4. l<u>ea</u>ving

1. made
2. late
3. hate
4. time
5. while

1. wait
2. rain
3. mail
4. tail

1. soak
2. coat

82

Waiting for a Pal

I hate to wait. I hate to sit in the rain. But I have to sit and wait while it rains.

I wait for my pal. My pal is the mail man.

The rain has made him late. That rain will soak my coat and my tail, but I will sit in the rain and wait.

At last I hear him and see him. I will run and jump. It's time for us to have lots of fun.

The end.

r   sh   ir   th   er   ur

1. h<u>ur</u>t
2. b<u>ur</u>n
3. b<u>ir</u>d
4. sh<u>ir</u>t

1. lots
2. robber
3. stopp<u>ed</u>

1. with
2. wish

1. soak
2. flame
3. more
4. time
5. side
6. here

1. near
2. ship
3. leap
4. barn

Bob was not confident.

A Mean Wind

Three pals made a fire near a farm. A mean wind made that fire leap over to the barn. The pals said, "We must hold this fire or the barn will go up in flames."

The mean wind said, "You can't stop this fire. I will blow big flames up the side of that barn."

But just as the flames began to
leap up the side of the barn, rain
came from the sky. Here is what
the rain said to the mean wind, "I
will keep those flames away from
the barn."

In no time, the fire was no more.

The rain told the wind, "Leave this farm or I will soak you some more."

The pals said, "We like rain."

But the mean wind said, "I hate rain."

This is the end.

133

1. f<u>ir</u>m
2. h<u>ur</u>t
3. sh<u>ir</u>t
4. d<u>ir</u>t

1. hot
2. shop
3. stopp<u>ed</u>

1. slide
2. what
3. goat
4. smiled
5. some
6. hit

1. robber
2. hidi<u>ng</u>
3. landed
4. rings
5. sn<u>ea</u>k

The Fast Rug

A hill had mud on it. A pig told a goat, "We can sit on my rug and slide on that hill. The rug will keep mud away from us."

So the goat and the pig sat on that rug. And the rug slid on the mud. The goat said, "This is a fast rug." A tree was in the way, and the rug hit the tree. The goat and the pig sailed into the sky and landed in the mud.

The goat said, "Now we have mud on us. So we can slide on the mud some more."

And that is what the goat and the pig did.

134

1. cop
2. rock
3. clock

1. Pam
2. lump
3. lamp
4. sn<u>ea</u>k
5. b<u>oa</u>t
6. hid<u>ing</u>

1. lit<u>tle</u>
2. <u>tur</u><u>tle</u>
3. bitt<u>er</u>
4. robbers

1. lip
2. rings
3. hunt
4. plan

Pam and the Gold Robber
Part One

Pam had a ship. <u>She</u> liv<u>ed</u> on that
ship. In h<u>er</u> ship, <u>she</u> had a shop.
The shop was fill<u>ed</u> with lots of
things.

One thing in that shop was lots of gold. Pam made gold rings and other gold things from the gold. But that gold was not in a big lump. Pam made the gold into some thing you see in a shop. That was her way of hiding the gold. She said, "My gold is now safe from robbers."

But one day a robber said, "I will
sneak into that ship and take the
gold from her shop."

This is not the end.

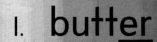

135

1. butt**er**
2. bitt**er**
3. lat**er**
4. aft**er**
5. litt**le**

1. cops
2. down
3. rocks
4. clocks

1. pick
2. sacks
3. lamp
4. plan
5. hunt
6. b**oa**t

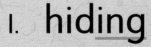

1. hidi**ng**
2. leavi**ng**
3. grabb**ed**

Pam and the Gold Robber
Part Two

A robber had a plan. He was going to sneak into Pam's ship and take her gold. He did not know that she had hid her gold. She had made the gold into some thing in her shop.

The robber got into his little boat. He waited as the sky got dark. He started to go to Pam's ship.

At last, the robber got to Pam's ship. He said, "Now I will grab a rope to go up the side of this ship and sneak into Pam's shop."

The robber did that. It was dark and still in the shop. The robber said, "Now I will hunt for the gold."

| More next time. |

136

1. bitt<u>er</u>
2. batt<u>er</u>
3. butt<u>er</u>
4. aft<u>er</u>
5. t<u>urtle</u>
6. l<u>ea</u>ving

1. ow
2. how
3. town
4. down
5. brown
6. mom

1. <u>sh</u>ow
2. throw
3. cl<u>ea</u>n
4. pick
5. sacks
6. meet

Pam and the Gold Robber
Part Three

Pam had a shop on h<u>er</u> ship. A robber got into h<u>er</u> shop to take the gold.

He said, "I see sacks and rocks and clocks. And I see a big lamp. But I see no gold."

At last, he gave up. Just as he was leaving, two cops came and grabbed him.

Later, the cops asked Pam, "Can you show us how you hide the gold?"

She said, "If you pick up the big lamp, you will know how I hide the gold."

One cop grabb**ed** the lamp. He said, "I can't pick up this lamp."

The **o**th**er** cop said, "I know <u>why</u> you can't pick it up. It's made of gold. Ho, ho, ho."

| The end. |

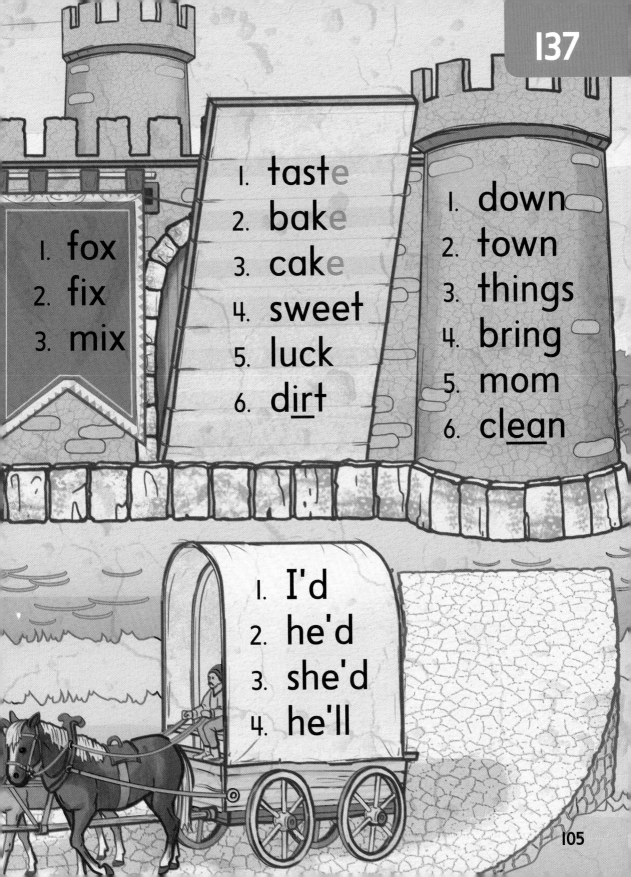

137

1. fox
2. fix
3. mix

1. taste
2. bake
3. cake
4. sweet
5. luck
6. d<u>ir</u>t

1. down
2. town
3. things
4. bring
5. mom
6. cl<u>ea</u>n

1. I'd
2. he'd
3. she'd
4. he'll

Sid Cleans Up the Town

Sid lik<u>ed</u> things that w<u>ere</u> cl<u>ea</u>n. But the town he liv<u>ed</u> in had lots of d<u>ir</u>t.

Sid told his mom, "I will make this town cl<u>ea</u>n."

His mom ask<u>ed</u>, "How will you do that?"

Sid said, "I will make it rain. The rain will cl<u>ea</u>n the d<u>ir</u>t away."

"But how will you make it rain?"

Sid said, "I will sing. What I sing will bring rain."

His mom said, "I don't think singing will make rain."

What I sing will bring rain.

I don't think so.

But Sid started to sing. In a little while, the sky got dark and lots of rain came down.

Sid's mom said, "I do not know what to think now."

Sid smiled and said, "I think the town is clean now."

And it was.

The end.

138

1. fox
2. box
3. mix

1. stopped
2. after
3. cake
4. back
5. luck
6. yuck

1. throw
2. brown
3. ca<u>sh</u>
4. taste

1. sweet
2. t<u>ur</u>t<u>l</u>es
3. bak<u>e</u>d
4. batter

109

Bitter Butter

Part One

A little turtle asked her mom to bake a cake. Her mom said, "We will need butter for the batter. So go to the farm and bring back some sweet butter."

She gave the little turtle some cash.

As the little turtle got near the farm, a brown fox stopped her. The fox asked her, "What do you plan to do with that cash?"

The little turtle told the fox that she needed sweet butter. The fox said, "You are in luck. I have some sweet butter." But the butter the fox had was bitter butter.

After the little turtle was on her way home,
the fox said, "Ho ho. I sold that bitter butter. So,
now I do not have to throw it away."

This is not the end.

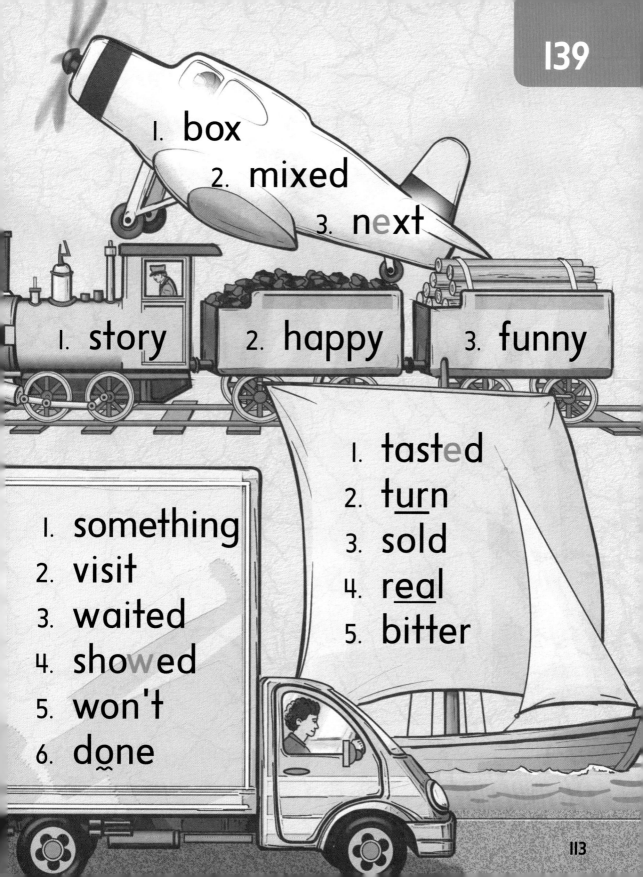

1. box
2. mixed
3. next

1. story
2. happy
3. funny

1. tasted
2. t<u>ur</u>n
3. sold
4. r<u>ea</u>l
5. bitter

1. something
2. visit
3. waited
4. sho<u>w</u>ed
5. won't
6. d<u>o</u>ne

Bitter Butter
Part Two

The brown fox had sold some bitter butter to the little turtle. Later, the little turtle came home with that butter.

Her mom showed her how to make a cake. Her mom said, "You start with cake batter."

Her mom began to make the batter. She said, "We mix sweet butter into the batter." But the butter she had was not sweet. It was bitter. And bitter butter won't make a sweet cake.

After the batter was made, the turtles waited while the cake baked. At last it was done.

The little turtle asked, "Can I taste that cake?"
"Yes," her mom said, and gave the little turtle
some cake.

The little turtle tasted the cake and said, "Yuck."

More next time.

1. wore
2. I'm
3. I've
4. here's
5. p<u>ay</u>
6. t<u>ur</u>n

1. only
2. tiny
3. funny
4. story
5. r<u>ea</u>lly

1. next
2. visit
3. drink
4. p<u>o</u>nd
5. f<u>ir</u>st
6. six

1. something
2. someone

Bitter Butter
Part Three

The little turtle tasted the cake. Did she like the taste? No. She said, "Mom, this cake is not sweet. It is bitter."

Her mom said, "How can the cake be bitter? The batter has fine things in it."

Her mom tasted the cake and said, "Yuck. That cake is bitter."

Her mom started to think. After a while she said, "Something bitter got into the cake batter. I think it was the butter. Bitter butter makes the batter bitter."

The little turtle's mom asked, "Who sold you this butter?"

The little turtle said, "The brown fox."

Her mom said, "We will go back and see him. I have something to say to him."

More next time.

142

1. <u>ea</u>ch
2. b<u>ea</u>ch
3. <u>ch</u>ase

1. m<u>o</u>ther
2. an<u>o</u>ther
3. visited
4. pond
5. dove
6. drink

1. n<u>ea</u>rly
2. d<u>ir</u>ty
3. r<u>ea</u>lly

1. bit
2. swim
3. thin
4. thinking
5. kids
6. glad

1. some<u>o</u>ne
2. something
3. inside

The cats relaxed on the grass.

Bitter Butter
Part Four

The next day, the mother turtle and the little turtle visited the brown fox. The turtles had a big cake.

The mother turtle told the fox, "We have a cake for you. But to have the cake, you have to show us that you like cake."

The fox liked things that were free, so he said, "I like it, I like it."

"You told us you like cake," the mother turtle said.

"But you have to <u>sh</u>ow us that you like it."

"How can I do that?" the fox asked.

The mother turtle said, "If you eat some cake r<u>ea</u>lly fast, we will know that you like it."

"I can do that," the fox said.

More to come.

143

1. shop
2. <u>ch</u>op
3. wish
4. whi<u>ch</u>
5. why
6. shake

1. baby
2. only
3. <u>ea</u>sy
4. n<u>ea</u>rly
5. body

1. dove
2. I'm
3. that's
4. wore
5. drink
6. visited

1. b<u>ea</u>t
2. began
3. sitting
4. wing
5. goes

Bitter Butter
Part Five

The mother turtle gave the fox some cake.
He ate it so fast that he didn't taste how bitter
it was. But after he was done, it started to leave
a bad taste.

"Did you like that?" the mother turtle asked.

"I . . . I . . ." the fox said. "I . . . need
something to drink."

The fox ran to the pond and dove in. He began to drink and drink, but the bad bitter taste did not go away.

"That cake is bitter," the fox said at last.

The mom asked, "Do you know why?"

The fox said, "Oh, it must be the butter I sold you."

The mother turtle said, "Yes, that bitter butter made the batter bitter."

The fox said, "And that bitter batter gave me a bitter taste."

That was the last time the fox sold someone bitter butter.

The end.

144

1. whale
2. ship
3. wish
4. whi<u>ch</u>
5. sh<u>a</u>rk
6. fish

1. carry
2. baby
3. <u>ea</u>sy
4. sleepy
5. body

1. br<u>o</u>ther
2. sister
3. winter
4. hunted
5. river
6. bigger

Fish

Fish swim in ponds, lakes, rivers, and seas. But lots of the things that swim in seas, rivers, ponds, and lakes are not fish.

You know what this is. What is it?
A seal is not a fish.

You know what this is. What is it?
Some turtles swim in lakes, seas, rivers, and ponds. But turtles are not fish.

This is a sh<u>ar</u>k. A sh<u>ar</u>k is a fish.

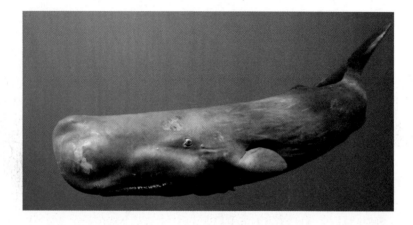

This is a whale. A whale is not a fish.

This is a goldfish. Is a goldfish a fish? Yes.

Some fish are big and some fish are little. Each fish starts as a little baby. Some of those baby fish grow into big, big fish. After sharks grow up, sharks are bigger than goldfish.

This fish is a whale shark. No other fish grows to be as big as a whale shark. The man next to the shark is six feet from end to end. Whale sharks can be up to 40 feet from end to end.

The end.

145

1. only
2. h<u>u</u>rry
3. tiny
4. thank
5. swim

1. sist<u>er</u>
2. l<u>ea</u>ves
3. <u>lea</u>ping
4. <u>si</u>tting
5. t<u>ur</u>n
6. f<u>ir</u>st

1. somebody
2. Jill
3. bite
4. br<u>o</u>ther
5. jumped

The Bug Who Bit
Part One

Jill was a bug who bit other bugs. That's why her brother and sister did not like to be near her.

One day she was playing with her brother and sister. The bugs were leaping over leaves.

Jill's sister jumped over three leaves. Her brother said, "Now it is my turn."

"No," Jill said. "It is my turn."

Her brother said, "I was here first. So it is my turn."

As he started to take his turn, he said, "Ow. Ow. Ow."

Why did he say that?

Somebody bit him.

Jill's brother and sister stopped playing. Her sister said, "We don't like to play with a bug who bites."

Her brother said, "Ow, I hurt."

So her brother and sister ran home.

Jill asked, "Why can't we play some more?"

More to come.

146

1. spring
2. snow
3. pants
4. winter
5. summer

1. I've
2. broke
3. chomp
4. bigger
5. glad
6. seen

1. reach
2. white
3. short
4. mark
5. thank
6. leaf

The Bug Who Bit

Part Two

Jill made her brother and sister mad. Her brother said, "Jill bites if things do not go her way."

One day, the bugs were at the pond. Her sister said, "Why don't we go for a swim?"

"Yes, yes," her brother said. "And we can dive from that tree."

"Oh no," Jill's sister said. "We don't know what is in that tree."

Jill said, "If something mean is in that tree, I will bite it."

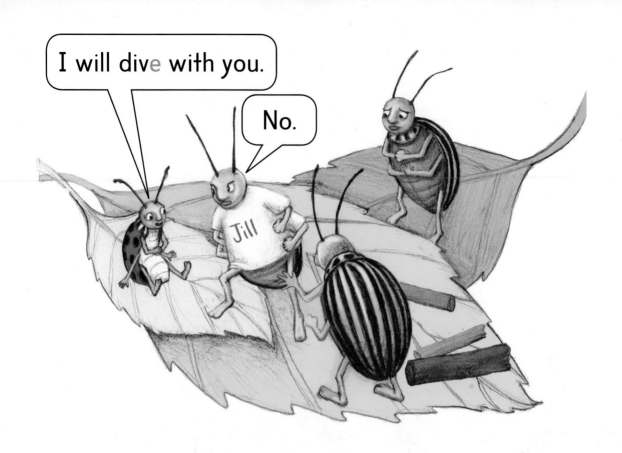

So the three bugs ran up the tree. The bugs
came to a little tiny bug who was sitting on a leaf.
That bug said, "What are you going to do?"

Jill's sister told him.

The little tiny bug said, "I like to dive. So I will
do it with you."

"No," Jill said. "Leave this tree or I will bite you."

This story is not over.

147

1. bite
2. beat
3. bit
4. before
5. broke
6. bigger

1. chomp
2. hard
3. mark
4. white
5. beach
6. hurry

1. hiking
2. diving
3. biting
4. kidding
5. thinking
6. wishing

I can bite really hard.

The Bug Who Bit

Part Three

Jill told the little bug to leave the tree. She said, "Go away, or I will bite you."

The little bug said, "That is a mean thing to do. I don't bite other bugs, but I can bite really hard if I have to."

That's how hard I can bite.

Jill said, "Ho ho. You think you can bite hard, but you can't beat me at biting."

Jill ran over to a stick and bit it. Her bite made a little mark on the stick.

The little bug ran over to another stick and bit it.
"CHOMP." His bite broke the stick.

Next he bit a bigger stick. "CHOMP." That stick
broke, too.

Jill's sister said, "You can bite like no other bug
I've seen."

Jill's brother said, "Yes, and I'm glad you don't
bite other bugs."

More next time.

1. bef<u>or</u>e
2. became
3. somebody
4. sunb<u>ur</u>n

1. diving
2. biting
3. thinking
4. kidding
5. sho<u>w</u>ing

1. sh<u>or</u>t
2. t<u>o</u>ld
3. st<u>or</u>y
4. st<u>or</u>m
5. r<u>o</u>lling
6. c<u>orn</u>

1. use
2. hotter
3. b<u>ir</u>ds
4. pants
5. h<u>ur</u>ry

The Bug Who Bit

Part Four

Jill had just seen a little tiny bug bite two sticks. The little bug said, "My mom told me not to be mean, so I try not to bite bugs. But, if a bug is really mean to me and makes me really mad, I bite."

Jill was thinking, "I will not make this bug mad at me." So Jill said, "I was just kidding before. I don't bite other bugs. That is a mean thing to do."

Jill's brother said, "Do you mean that, Jill?"

"Yes," Jill said. "Only a mean bug bites other bugs."

Later that day, the four bugs had lots of fun diving into the pond.

After that, one of the bugs said, "Why don't we go hiking?" And the bugs did that.

Those four bugs became pals. And from that day on, Jill did not bite other bugs.

The end.

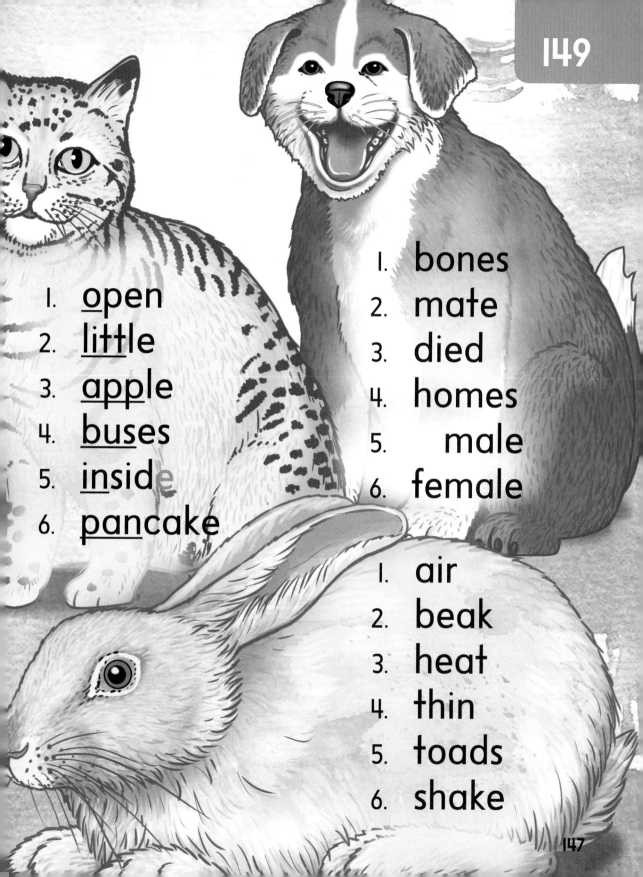

1. <u>o</u>pen
2. <u>litt</u>le
3. <u>a</u>pple
4. <u>bus</u>es
5. <u>in</u>side
6. <u>pan</u>cake

1. bones
2. mate
3. died
4. homes
5. male
6. female

1. air
2. beak
3. heat
4. thin
5. toads
6. shake

What Jan Sings

Jan liked to sing, but she made her mother sick of her singing.

One day her mother spoke to Jan. Her mother said, "I like the way you sing, but you sing the same thing over and over. Can you sing other things?"

Jan said, "I like to sing the same thing."

Her mother said, "I will do something for you if you sing more than one thing. What can I do for you?"

Jan said, "Will you sing with me?"

Jan's mom said, "Yes."

Now Jan and her mother sing lots of fine things.

If you are near Jan's home, you can hear that singing.

The end.

Sid Cleans Up the Town

Sid liked things that were clean. But the town he lived in had lots of dirt.

Sid told his mom, "I will make this town clean."

His mom asked, "How will you do that?"

Sid said, "I will make it rain. The rain will clean the dirt away."

"But how will you make it rain?"

Sid said, "I will sing. What I sing will bring rain."

His mom said, "I don't think singing will make rain."

But Sid started to sing. In a little while, the sky got dark and lots of rain came down.

Sid's mom said, "I do not know what to think now."

Sid smiled and said, "I think the town is clean now."

And it was.

The end.

1. winter
2. spring
3. shi__rt__s
4. b__ea__ch

1. your
2. six
3. week
4. bag
5. dock
6. black

1. they
2. ten
3. then
4. rent
5. went
6. left

1. __r__iding
2. __h__iding
3. __div__ing
4. __bit__ing

What Jan Makes
Part One

Jan liked to make things, but she made the same thing over and over. On one winter day, Jan's mom showed Jan how to make turtles from rocks.

Jan made the same turtle over and over. At last she had a pile of rock turtles.

Her mom said, "That pile is so big I can't see the rug. What are you going to do with these rock turtles?"

Jan said, "I will pile these turtles on the b<u>ea</u>ch. Kids can play on the pile of turtles."

Make a shi<u>r</u>t that is not the same.

On one spring day, Jan's mother showed Jan how to make a shi<u>r</u>t. Jan made five more shi<u>r</u>ts that were the same as the fi<u>r</u>st shi<u>r</u>t.

Jan's mom said, "You have lots of shi<u>r</u>ts that are the same. Why don't you make a shi<u>r</u>t for somebody other than you?"

"I will do that," Jan said. "I will make a shi<u>r</u>t for somebody who is bigger than I am."

More next time.

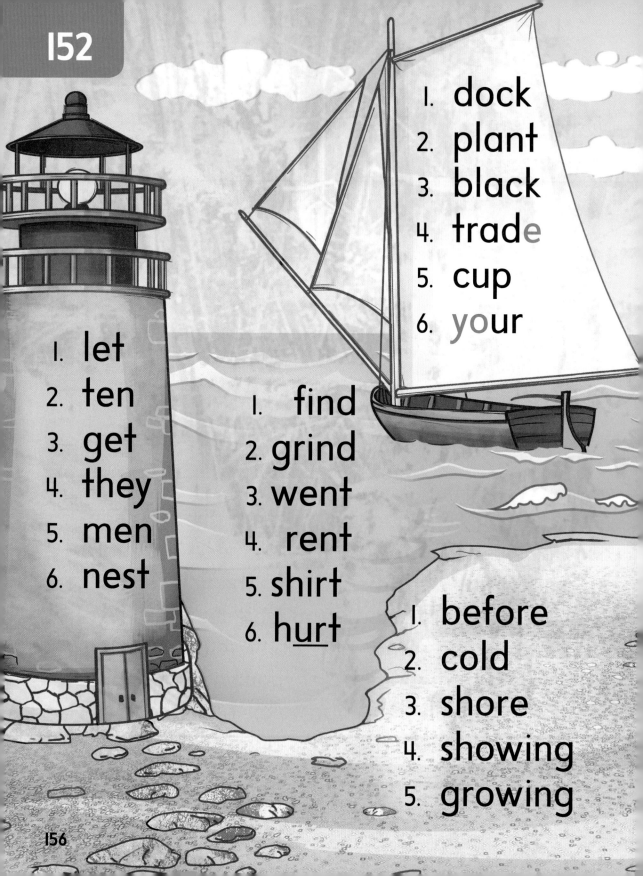

1. dock
2. plant
3. black
4. trade
5. cup
6. your

1. let
2. ten
3. get
4. they
5. men
6. nest

1. find
2. grind
3. went
4. rent
5. shirt
6. hurt

1. before
2. cold
3. shore
4. showing
5. growing

Six moms can fit in that shirt.

What Jan Makes
Part Two

Jan's mom showed her how to make a shirt. Jan made the same shirt five more times. After she had made those shirts, she told her mom that she was going to make a shirt for somebody who was bigger than she was.

Three days later, Jan showed that shirt to her mom. Jan's mom said, "This shirt is so big that six moms can fit in it."

Jan said, "I didn't know the shirt was going to be so big. What can we do with this shirt?"

"I think I know," Jan's mom said. "Come with me and I will show you." And she did.

Now, if you go by Jan's home, you m<u>ay</u> see what Jan and her mom did with that shirt. The shirt is on a car to keep dirt away. It seems to be a fine fit.

This story is over.

1. men
2. let's
3. left
4. when
5. went
6. get

1. wishing
2. fishing
3. tell
4. sell
5. find
6. kind

1. <u>boat</u>ing
2. <u>swim</u>ming
3. <u>kit</u>ten
4. <u>start</u>ed
5. <u>fe</u>male
6. <u>bet</u>ter

1. lake
2. nine
3. day
4. store
5. each

Ten Men

Ten men liked to do things with each other. When one man went to a show, the other nine men went with him. When one man went to the store, the other nine men went with him.

One day, a man said, "Let's go fishing."

The other nine men said, "Yes, let's go fishing."

So ten men got in a van, and away they went to the lake.

When they got to the lake, the men said, "We will rent a boat." And they did.

Only one boat was left, and it was not a big boat. It was made for three men, not ten men.

The first three men said, "We will get in this boat." And they did.

As they started to leave the dock, the other men said, "We will get in this boat, too." And they did.

Did the boat hold the men? No.

So the ten men did not go boating and did not go fishing. Those men went swimming.

The end.

154

1. them
2. bed
3. pens
4. red
5. mess
6. when

1. year
2. traded
3. planted
4. sleeping
5. kittens

1. rid
2. sale
3. much
4. Debby
5. week
6. cups

1. five
2. two
3. piles
4. next
5. grows

Debby Makes Trades
Part One

Debby liked to trade things. She was a fine trader. She said, "When I trade, I end up with more than I had before."

One week, she traded her bike for other things. She got another bike and a sleeping bag and some cash.

She traded the sleeping bag for a cat that had nine kittens.

She traded the kittens for lots and lots of other things. She ended up with her cat, a bird, a ring, three pens, five fish, six cups, two clocks, and the bike she had at first.

She made another trade for some ears of corn. This corn was not gold like other corn. This corn was red, and brown, and black, and white. She traded some of the corn and planted some of the corn.

The next year, she had piles and piles of corn. Her mom's pals liked that corn. So Debby made a lot of trades.

More next time.

155

1. much
2. rid
3. rugs
4. mess
5. bed
6. them

1. fine
2. sale
3. may
4. these

1. white
2. trade
3. trading
4. named
5. opened

1. stays
2. lays
3. tell
4. sell
5. three
6. free

Debby Makes Trades
Part Two

Debby planted some corn that was not gold. It was red, and brown, and black, and white. The corn came up the next year, and Debby made lots of trades. After she was done trading, her home was a mess.

Debby had piles of things on the rugs and piles of things on her bed. At last her mom said, "You must get rid of these things."

Debby said, "But when I trade, I get more than I had before."

Her mom said, "I will tell you how to get rid of these things. Sell them."

Debby said, "That is a fine plan."
So Debby had a sale, and it was a big one.
When the sale was over, Debby had three ears of corn, two pens, one fish, and one big pile of cash.

Debby had so much cash that she opened a store. It is named Debby's. Debby will sell or trade. So if you have things you don't need, you may make a trade with Debby.

The end.

1. apples
2. animals
3. feathers
4. pictures
5. better
6. funny

1. of
2. off
3. their
4. live

1. class
2. nest
3. pop
4. pod
5. wing
6. flap

1. eggs
2. legs
3. beans
4. cleans
5. pet
6. wet

1. males
2. bones
3. beaks
4. die
5. air
6. mate
7. goes

173

Birds

One class of animals is birds.

Each bird has two legs, two wings, one beak, and lots of feathers.

The heat of a bird's body stays the same when the air is hot and when the air is cold. The body heat of bugs, snakes, and toads goes up when the air is hot and it goes down when the air is cold.

A lot of birds have bones that are filled with <u>ai</u>r. These birds can fly.

Birds with bones filled with more than <u>ai</u>r can't fly.

This bird can't fly, but it can run with a man on it.

In the spring, birds find a mate. Male birds may do funny things to find a mate. One thing male birds do is show off to female birds. The male birds sing, flap th<u>ei</u>r wings, and shake th<u>ei</u>r tail f<u>ea</u>thers.

This male bird is showing off to the female. Female birds pick the male that shows off better than other males. Those two birds will live with <u>ea</u>ch other.

The two birds make a nest. A little while later, the female lays up to ten eggs. Each egg has a baby bird in it.

157

1. beans
2. cob
3. plants
4. pods
5. use
6. well
7. wheat
8. milk

1. many
2. popcorn
3. powder
4. pancakes
5. kernels

1. cook
2. rice
3. bread
4. picture
5. off

1. their
2. where
3. there
4. finds
5. grinds
6. kinds

178

Bird Nests

A lot of birds make nests before they mate. Some birds make the<u>ir</u> nests in grass. Some birds make the<u>ir</u> nests in trees. Some birds like trees that have died. Other birds like trees that have not died.

Here are pictures of some birds and the<u>ir</u> nests.

Some birds live in homes made for birds. Some birds make nests in homes like your home. And some birds live in nests made by other birds.

Some mother birds can l<u>ay</u> up to ten eggs.

The birds sit on their eggs so the eggs won't get cold. If an egg gets too cold, the baby bird inside it will die.

Male and female birds take turns sitting on the eggs. The bird that is not sitting on the eggs hunts for things to eat.

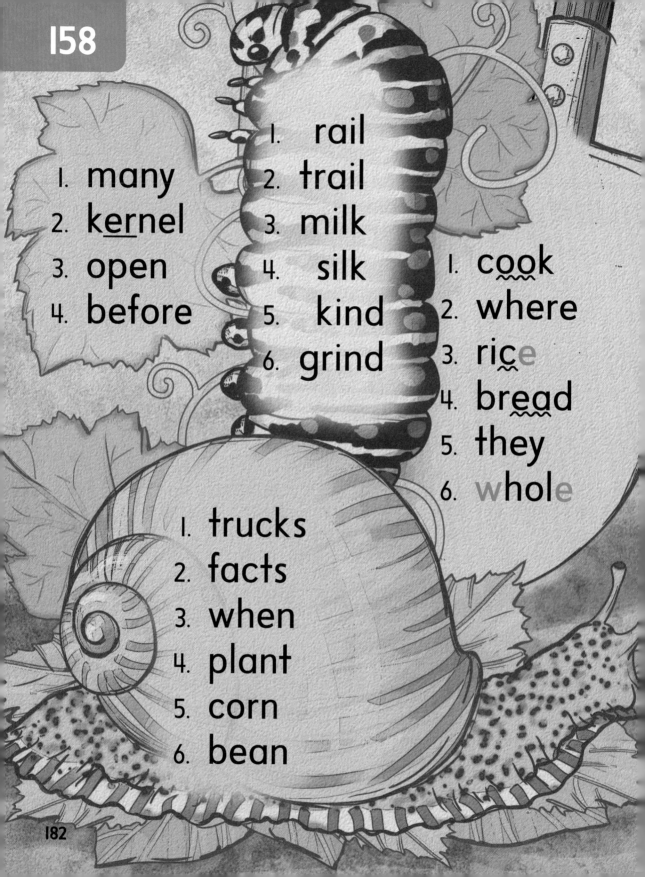

1. rail
2. trail
3. milk
4. silk
5. kind
6. grind

1. many
2. kernel
3. open
4. before

1. cook
2. where
3. rice
4. bread
5. they
6. whole

1. trucks
2. facts
3. when
4. plant
5. corn
6. bean

Seeds

These are things we eat. They are seeds that grow on plants.

These are beans. The beans are seeds. Beans grow in pods. Pods grow on bean plants. How many seeds are in the pod that is open?

We cook a lot of beans before we eat them.

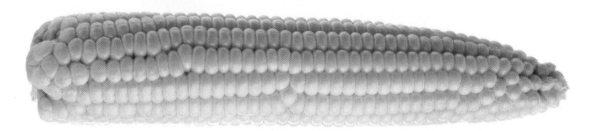

These seeds are corn. Corn seeds are kernels of corn. There are many kernels on a corn cob.

Corn plants grow corn. The corn cob grows inside green leaves. This whole thing is an ear of corn.

We cook a lot of corn before we eat it.

Some corn has kernels that pop when they get hot. That kind of corn is popcorn.

Beans and corn are seeds. So if you plant them, they will grow into bean plants or corn plants.

Here's a bean planted in a little hole.

Here's a bean plant when it first starts to grow.

Here's the plant when it is bigger.

Here's the plant when it has bean pods on it.

1. mix
2. use
3. wh<u>ea</u>t
4. wet
5. well

1. ri<u>c</u>e
2. ni<u>c</u>e
3. c<u>oo</u>k
4. b<u>oo</u>k
5. then
6. when

1. many
2. br<u>ea</u>d
3. kind
4. picture

1. l<u>oa</u>ded
2. buses
3. apples
4. powd<u>er</u>
5. <u>rea</u>lly
6. pancakes

1. <u>ai</u>r
2. goes
3. grass
4. plane
5. whole

What kind of seeds are in this ear?

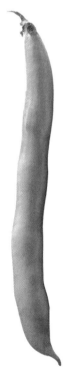

What kind of seeds are in this pod?

Grass Seeds

There are many kinds of grass. You can eat the seeds of some kinds of grass.

These plants are kinds of grass.

Grass with these seeds is wheat. We don't eat the other parts of this grass, just the seeds.

We use wheat seeds to make bread. We dry wheat seeds and grind up part of each kernel to make a powder.

Then we mix that powder with eggs and milk to make things like pancakes and bread.

Here are wh<u>ea</u>t k<u>er</u>nels
planted on dirt.

Here are the plants when
they first start to grow.

Here are the plants when
they have wh<u>ea</u>t k<u>er</u>nels on
them.

Grass with these seeds is rice. Rice plants grow well in dirt that is really wet.

Here's a rice plant in wet dirt.

Here's the plant when it has rice kernels on it.

We cook the rice kernels before we eat them.